HOW RAILROADS SHAPED AMERICA

Jack O'Mara

New York

Published in 2009 by The Rosen Publishing Group, Inc.
29 East 21st Street, New York, NY 10010

Book Design: Haley W. Harasymiw

Photo Credits: Cover © Richard Sargeant/Shutterstock; p. 5 © Yusef El-Mansouri/Shutterstock; pp. 6, 9, 11, 12 (Dodge), 13, 17, 19, 21 © Hulton Archive/Getty Images; p. 10 http://en.wikipedia.org/wiki/Image:US_Civil_War_railway_gun_and_crew.jpg; p. 12 (Judah) http://en.wikipedia.org/wiki/Image:Theodore_Judah.jpg; pp. 14, 20 © Time & Life Pictures/Getty Images; p. 22 http://en.wikipedia.org/wiki/Image:1876_B%260.jpg; p. 23 © Jeff Williams/Shutterstock; p. 24 © Thomas Barrat/Shutterstock; p. 25 http://en.wikipedia.org/wiki/Image:NYC_subway_map.png; p. 26 © Getty Image News/Getty Images; p. 28 http://en.wikipedia.org/wiki/Image:SNCF_TGV-A_359_at_Poitiers _Futuroscope.JPG; p. 29 http://en.wikipedia.org/wiki/Image:JR-Maglev-MLX01-2.jpg.

Library of Congress Cataloging-in-Publication Data

O'Mara, Jack.
  How railroads shaped America / Jack O'Mara.
      p. cm. - (Real life readers)
  Includes index.
  ISBN: 978-1-4358-0175-2 (paperback)
  6-pack ISBN: 978-1-4358-0176-9
  ISBN 978-1-4358-2993-0 (library binding)
  1. Railroads—United States—History—19th century—Juvenile literature. I. Title.
  TF23.O53 2009
  385.0973-dc22

                              2008039107

CONTENTS

HOW DO WE GET THERE?

We live in a busy, fast world. Whenever we need to **communicate** with someone, we can instantly send them a text message or use our cell phones. When we need to get somewhere, we often look for the fastest way to travel. If it's only a few miles away, we may take a car. To travel a great distance, we may fly on a plane. Trains are another way for people to reach near and far **destinations**.

Every day, millions of people take trains that travel above or under the ground all around large cities. Other trains carry passengers across the country. Although trains are not used as much as cars today, they were once the most popular and important form of **transportation**. In fact, trains and the U.S. railroad system changed American lives forever. Let's find out how.

How do you get from place to place?
Have you ever taken a train?

To Union Station

Animals such as horses and mules powered early railroads. Some inventors even tried to use sails for wind-powered trains! In 1804, an English inventor named Richard Trevithick used a steam engine to move a four-wheeled cart along a track. This was the first steam **locomotive**. Even more amazing was the fact that the cart was

The 1830 race between the Tom Thumb and the horse-drawn railroad car, shown here, inspired many inventors to build better trains. The first steam powered passenger rail service began that same year.

able to pull 10 tons (9 metric tons) of iron, seventy men, and five wagons! This was much more than any horse-drawn cart could manage.

Soon, engineers in the United States were building steam locomotives. The most successful was Peter Cooper. In 1830, he constructed a steam engine that was smaller than earlier ones but just as powerful. Cooper used it to power a locomotive called the Tom Thumb. A race between the Tom Thumb and a horse-drawn cart drew a lot of attention. The locomotive was faster than the horse until the engine broke down near the end of the race.

definition:	details:
a self-powered form of transportation that pulls or pushes railroad cars in a train	• word comes from Latin words meaning "place" and "moving" • many pull or push cars carrying passengers or goods • different locomotives have different power sources

locomotive

examples:	non-examples:
• steam locomotives • electric locomotives • **diesel** locomotives	• railroad car • airplane • horse-drawn train

By 1835, more than 200 railroad companies existed in the United States. Nearly 1,000 miles (1,600 km) of track had been laid. This number jumped to over 15,000 miles (24,000 km) by 1854! All states east of the Mississippi River had railroads, with most of the track connecting large northeastern cities. Railroad lines became important trade routes. A number of small railroad companies **merged** to form larger companies that carried greater amounts of people and goods.

In the mid-1800s, much of the midwestern and southwestern United States was still unsettled. The government saw how quickly trains could transport people from place to place. They offered railroad companies land to build tracks through less-populated areas. Just as they hoped, the new railroad lines drew settlers to these regions. The railroad was helping the United States to grow.

The discovery of gold near Sacramento, California, in 1848 made people look for new ways of transportation across the United States. Before trains, people took months to travel between the East and West Coasts in stagecoaches similar to the one shown here.

THE RACE ACROSS THE COUNTRY

In 1861, the **American Civil War** broke out. Railroads played an important part in the Northern victory. Most of the railroad tracks had been built around the factories and businesses in the North rather than the farm-based communities of the South. Therefore, the North had more trains to carry soldiers, weapons, and supplies where they were needed.

Even before the war started, some people began planning a project that would change the United States forever. On July 1, 1862,

This photo shows Southern soldiers transporting a gun during the American Civil War.

President Abraham Lincoln signed the Pacific Railroad Act to further encourage the growth of the country. This act created the Union Pacific Railroad Company, which began laying tracks westward from the Missouri River. The Central Pacific Railroad Company was chosen to lay tracks eastward from Sacramento, California. The Pacific Railroad Act gave both of the businesses government land and money to complete a **transcontinental** railroad.

President Abraham Lincoln

One of the biggest problems encountered while planning the transcontinental railroad was finding the best route. Fortunately, Grenville Dodge—a railroad worker who had long supported the idea of a cross-country track—had scouted a westward route in the 1850s. It followed paths used for many years by Cheyenne and Sioux Indians that ran along rivers and through the Rocky Mountains.

The Union Pacific Railroad planned to follow Dodge's route. Theodore Judah of the Central Pacific Railroad succeeded in the difficult task of finding a way eastward through the Sierra Nevada mountain range. Both Dodge and Judah made sure their trails were wide and flat enough for railroad tracks.

Grenville Dodge

Theodore Judah

With the route set, it was time to build. Each company realized that, under the Pacific Railroad Act, the more track it laid, the more land and money it would receive from the government. The race to lay the most railroad track began!

This Union Pacific Railroad poster from 1867 advertises a new section of track connecting Omaha and North Platte, Nebraska.

THE SHORTEST AND QUICKEST ROUTE
BETWEEN THE
MOUNTAINS AND THE EAST
IS VIA THE

UNION PACIFIC R.R
NOW OPEN FROM
OMAHA TO NORTH PLATTE
300 Miles West of the Missouri River, and 200 Miles nearer Denver and Salt Lake than any other Railroad Line.

All Passenger Trains of this Road Connect Direct
WITH TRAINS OF THE
CHICAGO & NORTH-WESTERN R'Y, WHICH IS NOW COMPLETED FROM
CHICAGO TO OMAHA
Making 800 Miles of Railroad directly West of Chicago with but "One Change of Cars."

PASSENGERS CROSSING THE PLAINS
Will save 200 Miles Stage Travel and 48 Hours Time by taking this Route.
PULLMAN'S PALACE SLEEPING CARS ON ALL NIGHT TRAINS
Equipment all new, and Road bed in perfect order. Good Eating Houses at convenient points on line.

DIRECT CONNECTIONS MADE AT NORTH PLATTE WITH WELLS, FARGO & CO'S DAILY LINES OF
OVERLAND MAIL AND EXPRESS COACHES
To and from Denver, Central City, Salt Lake, and ALL POINTS in Colorado, Utah, Idaho, Montana, Nevada and California.

PASSENGERS, TO AVAIL THEMSELVES OF THE QUICK TIME AND SURE CONNECTIONS OF THIS ROUTE, MUST
Ask for Tickets via Omaha.

THE ATTENTION OF SHIPPERS OF FREIGHT FOR THE MOUNTAINS
Is particularly called to the opening of the great Platte Valley Route to NORTH PLATTE, and its connections. 200 Miles of Wagon Transportation is saved in sending Goods via OMAHA. Reliable Freight Lines are at all times prepared to transport Goods from the Western terminus of this Road to all points in the Mountains. Careful handling and quick time guaranteed.
RATES ALWAYS AS LOW AND CHANGES FEWER THAN BY ANY OTHER ROUTE.

W. SNYDER, Gen'l Fr't and Ticket Agent.   SAM'L B. REED, Gen'l Superintendent.

This picture from 1866 shows Union Pacific worker Samuel Reed checking the route before track was laid in Omaha.

Building the transcontinental railroad wasn't an easy process. Even with help from the government, both companies had problems raising funds. The Pacific Railroad Act of 1864 eased the financial strain.

Each company employed thousands of workers to do risky, backbreaking work. Workers cleared away trees, rocks, and soil. They blasted tunnels through mountains. They laid wood ties side by side. Then, they placed heavy iron rails on the ties. Each rail weighed about 700 pounds (318 kg)! Finally, they hammered the rails into place with iron spikes.

Much of the land on which the workers laid track was home to Native Americans. Angry that their land was being taken over, some Native Americans attacked workers.

On May 10, 1869, the Union Pacific and Central Pacific workforces finally met at Promontory Summit, Utah. Leaders from both railroads joined the two tracks with a golden spike. With a final tap, railroad track connected the West and East Coasts.

This route changed American lives forever. Until that time, taking a stagecoach or wagon across country could take 6 months and cost about $1,000. Now a person could travel across country in 1 week for about $65. With a fast, dependable way to travel, many more people were willing to go west and settle all across the United States.

The transcontinental railroad brought many changes to communication as well. Before, a letter traveling by horse or wagon cost several dollars to send, which many people couldn't afford. After, mail sent by train cost just pennies. Also, the first transcontinental **telegraph** line had been constructed along the rails. Now messages could be sent across the country in a matter of minutes!

At the final spike ceremony, shown here, the message "DONE" was sent by telegraph to the East and West Coasts. By the end of the 1800s, the United States had five transcontinental railroads!

LIFE ALONG THE RAILS

The transcontinental railroad and other railroad lines did more than take people to destinations. They helped create towns and cities. Communities grew up along the tracks and encouraged trains to stop so passengers could use their shops, hotels, restaurants, and other businesses. Some towns lasted only a short time while railroad workers were around. A few towns became well known for crime and wild behavior. However, other small towns,

CAUSE:

The transcontinental railroad connected the West and East Coasts of the United States.

↓

EFFECTS:

- Settlers moved to less-populated parts of the country.
- Goods and communication traveled easily, inexpensively, and quickly from place to place.
- Towns and cities were established and grew larger along railroads.

such as Cheyenne, Wyoming, drew a large number of settlers and grew into large cities that still exist today.

Existing towns and cities often requested that railroad routes stopped there. A railway stop meant more business, trade, and people. It basically assured the growth and **prosperity** of a community.

This picture from 1971 shows a Union Pacific train waiting at the railway station in Cheyenne, Wyoming.

The Pullman Palace Car Company was the largest employer of African Americans in the early 1900s. Being a Pullman porter—or a worker who assists passengers with their bags—was one of the best-paying jobs for African Americans at the time.

CHANGES IN TRAINS

During the time that railroads expanded across the country, trains changed inside and out. The first passenger trains were open to the air, which meant people were exposed to the weather. Later, windows were added so people were protected from the weather, but they could still see outside. In 1867, the Pullman Palace Car Company built sleeper cars so passengers could rest on long rides. Many trains had grand dining rooms as well.

Train safety was also an issue. The first train brakes were pulled by hand. Many trains had accidents if the brake wasn't applied while a train went around a curve. It also took a long time for the train to come to a complete stop. In 1869, American inventor George Westinghouse constructed one of the first railroad **air brakes**, which made stopping a lot faster and safer.

In the late 1800s, iron railroad tracks were replaced by longer-lasting steel tracks. Steel cars replaced wood trains and became faster and more powerful. By the 1890s, people had found ways to use

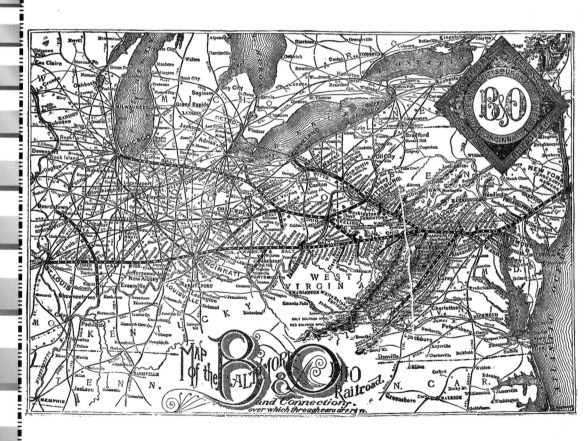

In 1895, the Baltimore and Ohio Railroad used the first electric
locomotive in the United States.

electricity to run locomotives. Steam locomotives began to be replaced by diesel-electric locomotives beginning in the 1930s.

Trains continued to be popular during **World War II**, especially since many people didn't have the money or fuel to drive. However, after the war, people began to drive cars more and use airplanes to travel to distant places. Railroad companies lost money even with government aid. Finally, in 1970, the U.S. government helped form and fund Amtrak, a business that merged almost all U.S. passenger train companies. Amtrak still exists today.

THE RISE OF RAPID TRANSIT

As U.S. cities continued to grow, the places where people lived and worked grew farther apart. A new railway system presented a convenient way for people to get around. "Rapid transit" refers to a system of electric trains that provides transportation many times a day to a large number of people in an **urban** area. Some of these trains travel on the ground like regular trains. Some travel underground, and some are elevated above street level.

The largest and busiest rapid transit system in the United States

The oldest sections of the elevated train in Chicago, Illinois, date back to 1892.

is the New York City Subway, which opened in 1904. It has over 650 miles (1,050 km) of track. It runs 24 hours a day, 365 days a year, and carries more people than any other transit system in the United States.

Rapid transit is usually an inexpensive way to travel, and it helps reduce the amount of traffic on city streets. Many people also use this form of public transportation because it produces less pollution than cars and buses.

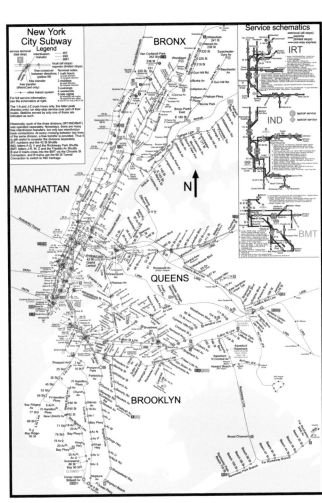

This is a map of the New York City Subway system.

Rapid transit trains make many stops in a city. Commuter trains are trains that travel between cities and nearby towns. They don't run as often or have as many stops. Rapid transit systems work together with commuter trains to make distant communities easier to get to. Many rapid transit and commuter trains have the added advantage of traveling much faster than cars, and they don't need to stop at signs or lights as often as road traffic.

Trains have not only changed the way the United States looks, but also the way that Americans live. Years ago, people in a city might not have ever traveled to another city 100 miles (161 km) away. Now, many people use trains to travel this distance several times a week to work, visit friends and family, or attend a concert!

Amtrak's Acela trains are currently the fastest trains in the United States. They are capable of reaching speeds up to 150 miles (241 km) per hour.

Railroads today still hold many advantages over other methods of transportation. Large cities often experience rush-hour traffic on busy roads. Train lines don't have as much traffic to deal with. Trains create less air pollution than airplanes and most cars.

Traveling by train is a pleasant way to see the country! Railroad tracks are laid across wide plains, through snow-topped

French TGV

The French TGV train is the fastest wheeled train, traveling 357 miles (574 km) per hour, just a bit slower than the Japanese JR-Maglev.

Japanese JR-Maglev

mountain ranges, and across mighty rivers. Travelers may not always see these sights from busy highways or high in the air.

In recent years, there have been some amazing engineering breakthroughs for trains. One kind of train in Japan—the JR-Maglev—uses electrical and magnetic forces to float the train above the track! In 2003, it became the fastest form of ground transportation. The JR-Maglev's top speed is 361 miles (581 km) per hour! Someday soon, newer trains may move even faster.

TIMELINE OF RAILROADS IN THE UNITED STATES

—1830—Peter Cooper develops the steam locomotive Tom Thumb; first passenger service starts.

—1835—About 1,000 miles (1,600 km) of railroad tracks exist in the United States.

—1854—Over 15,000 miles (24,000 km) of railroad tracks exist in the United States.

—1862—President Abraham Lincoln signs the Pacific Railroad Act.

—1867—The Pullman Palace Car Company builds sleeper cars with beds.

—1869—Union Pacific and Central Pacific Railroads meet in Promontory Summit, Utah, to complete the first transcontinental railroad; George Westinghouse builds one of the first railroad air brakes.

—1892—First elevated sections of Chicago's rapid transit system are constructed.

—1895—Baltimore and Ohio Railroad provides the first U.S. railroad service using an electric locomotive.

—1904—New York City Subway begins service.

—1970—U.S. government helps railroad companies merge into Amtrak.

GLOSSARY

air brake (EHR BRAYK) A brake that uses air pressure to stop a wheel on a train.

American Civil War (uh-MEHR-uh-kuhn SIH-vuhl WOHR) A war between the Northern and Southern states of the United States from 1861 to 1865.

communicate (kuh-MYOO-nuh-kayt) To share facts or feelings.

destination (dehs-tuh-NAY-shun) A place to which a person travels.

diesel (DEE-zuhl) An oil commonly used to power certain kinds of engines.

locomotive (loh-kuh-MOH-tihv) A car capable of moving itself that runs on tracks and pulls or pushes train cars.

merge (MUHRJ) To combine two or more things to make a single thing.

prosperity (prah-SPEHR-uh-tee) The condition of having great wealth or success.

telegraph (TEH-luh-graf) A machine used to send messages through wires using coded signals.

transcontinental (trans-kahn-tuh-NEHN-tuhl) Going across a continent.

transportation (trans-puhr-TAY-shun) A way of traveling from one place to another.

urban (UHR-buhn) Having to do with a city.

World War II (WUHRLD WOHR TOO) A war fought in Europe, Africa, and Asia from 1939 to 1945.

INDEX

Due to the changing nature of Internet links, The Rosen Publishing Group, Inc., has developed an online list of Web sites related to the subject of this book. This site is updated regularly. Please use this link to access the list: http://www.rcbmlinks.com/rlr/railr